Duh…

Capitalism

Observations from your

average 54 year old

American.

Definition of Capitalism:

An economic and political system
in which a country's trade and
industry are controlled by
private owners for profit
rather than by the state.

Definition of Socialism:

A political and economic theory
of social organization that
advocates that the means of
production, distribution and
exchange should be owned
or regulated by the state.

Table of Contents

Capitalism

Capitalism values the individual.

That is you !

Capitalism functions to make sure

you are satisfied as a consumer and

rewarded as a worker.

It is up to you, the individual

to pursue your own happiness.

Socialism

The state is more important than the individual.

Capitalism

Freedom is necessary for capitalism to thrive.

Since the individual is in control, free markets are the most efficient system to create, produce and distribute goods and services.

Socialism

The state needs to control the individual.

Freedom is diminished in favor of regulations and high taxes.

Capitalism

Capitalism provides incentives
for individuals in their pursuit of
happiness.

No outcomes are guaranteed,
but opportunities are limitless.

Socialism

In order for the state to keep
control – taxes must be high.

Taxes influence behavior.
The more you tax something
the more you reduce its result.

High taxes reduce the incentive
for the individual to work.

Capitalism

Profits are good and necessary.

Profits are the incentive that encourage behavior needed to produce goods and services.

Excess profits are put back into the economy, community and charity.

Socialism

Socialism views profits as a

form of oppression and corruption.

High taxes are preferred over profits.

Excess taxes are controlled by

politicians and bureaucrats

and used as a tool

to keep their power.

Capitalism

Capitalism rewards a strong
work ethic.

You reap what you sow.

Socialism

The work ethic is neutralized

since non-work is rewarded.

Capitalism

**Wealth is created in the process
of satisfying the individual.**

Socialism

Wealth is confiscated by the state

from those who created it and

distributed to those

who didn't.

Capitalism

The greatest social program

is a job.

The incentive to earn profits and
wealth, creates jobs.

Jobs offer dignity and hope.

They provide a pathway to wealth.

Socialism

The incentive to increase wealth
is diminished by the states
regulatory control.

High regulations and high taxes
reduce jobs.

Capitalism

Capitalism thrives when the government is small.

Small government enhances the power of the individual.

The smaller the government the bigger the individual.

Socialism

The state thrives as the
government gets bigger.

Bigger government means
more regulation, more taxes,
more corruption and more poverty.

Those of us who earned an allowance by doing household chores will understand:

Capitalism will let you keep all of your allowance for your work. If you work harder you can earn a bigger allowance resulting with a clean house.

Socialism will take a portion of your allowance and give it to those who don't do household chores. You will now work less or not at all – and your house will be in ruins.

Socialism

Bigger government = Less freedom

Less freedom = Less incentive

Less incentive = Less profits

Less profits = Less jobs

Less jobs = MORE POVERTY

MORE SOCIALISM = MORE DESPAIR

Capitalism

Smaller government = More freedom

More freedom = More incentive

More incentive = More profits

More profits = More jobs

More jobs = LESS POVERTY

MORE CAPITALISM = MORE PROSPERITY

Summary

Socialism

Socialism has no incentive or mechanism to create wealth.

It can only increase poverty in the world.

You can't help a citizen by punishing another.

As poverty increases – the state control over the individual increases.

Summary

<u>Capitalism</u>

Capitalism is the greatest
invention in the history of the world.

It is the only solution to minimize
poverty and maximize prosperity.

It is not a theory and it has worked
where ever it is implemented.

What is your world view
for the future?

Conclusion

Duh...

CAPITALISM !

Made in the USA
Las Vegas, NV
22 September 2021